The Man, the Boy and the Tamarisk Tree

Tess Driver

The Man, the Boy and the Tamarisk Tree

Acknowledgements

Previously published:
'Watching Friends on a Wet Day
'Teapot'
'Death is a White Syntax'
'Road kill'
'El Duende'
'Backyard Bird'
'Solitary at Sea'
'One Day at Notre Dame'
'White Crane'
'Sonnet For John'

The Man, the Boy and the Tamarisk Tree
ISBN 978 1 76109 549 8
Copyright © text Tess Driver 2023
Cover image from Pixabay

First published 2023 by
GINNINDERRA PRESS
PO Box 3461 Port Adelaide 5015
www.ginninderrapress.com.au

Contents

Aphrodisiac	7
Warning	8
Party Dress	9
Elephant in His Pocket	10
Stones	11
Deceived By Appearances	12
Watching Friends on a Wet Day	13
Teapot	14
Black Bear	15
Death is a White Syntax	17
The Black Hole of Three A.M.	18
Solitary Man	19
Elephantidae Loxodonta Africana	20
Scattered	21
The Silent Place	22
The Last Dahlia	23
2 The Last Dahlia	24
Dancing With the Tide	25
The Lost Children of Bangkok	26
Blossom Time	27
The Power of Silence	28
Tombstone, Arizona	29
Apple Pie	30
Before Full Moon	31
Criticism	32
Eggshells	33
Road Kill	34
No More Vintage	35
Moments	36
El Duende	37

Sunday Benediction	38
Backyard Bird	39
Solitary at Sea	40
Taksu	41
Too Many Goodbyes	42
Grandma's Garden	43
Boy at the Bus Stop	44
Devil Mixed With Angels	45
Argonauta Nodosa	46
White Crane	47
Sonnet For John	48
The Singer	49
An Insubstantial Sweetness	50
One Day at Notre Dame	51
Mellow Season	52
The Tamarisk	53
Drown in Birdsong	54
The Housewife	55
Sometimes She Understands the Right Thing at the Right Time	56
Roots	57
Sing My Poem	58
Summer Evening	59
The Children Sing	60
Driftwood	62
A Rose By Name	63

Aphrodisiac

Climb inside, comfort me
with lush imaginings as I
walk the tightrope of your lines.

I caress the lips of your knowing.
Read to me poet, soothe my imaginings,
massage my longing with thoughts
that cling to every pore.

I shiver at your rhyme;
it is dark outside, poet,
fill me with light and laughter
so the moon grows full and stars
caress the nippled dawn.

Poet, lust after me
with your singing verse:
wash the sharp word edges,
drown me in the flesh of your verse.

Warning

Clouds are building,
macabre faces hang grey and heavy.
Below, the sea shivers,
rumbles onto grinding stones.
Long-winged birds glide
challenge a warning wind,
wires begin to dance
from pole to pole.
Giant drops fall, splat on hot bitumen.

She sighs, too wet to walk the dog,
curls like a thought in the sagging armchair.
Easier to contemplate obligations than
succumb to the downpour of realities.

Party Dress

Fragile as the truth
it hangs on a crocheted hook
covered in white blossom,
a gossamer memory.
All that time,
season to season
green embroidered petals
now pale and frayed
danced on cream silk,
styled with tucks for secrets.
So slim, two large hands
could fit around the waist.
Kisses flutter moth-like
from the neckline
once softly curved
over quivering breasts.
A million silken threads
to create a dream.
Touch it gently
or it will unravel
in your hands.

Elephant in His Pocket

'I am hurrying,' his granddaughter said. She was burrowing now. 'Where did you put them, Pa?' Small hands felt in sagging pockets but only dusty memories stuck to her groping fingers. 'No teeth there. You're falling to pieces, Grandpa.' 'Like an old savannah elephant,' he sighed. 'It's time I found my resting place.' 'Look, what's this?' she cried. In the pocket of his cardigan grazed an elephant with tusks. He trumpeted, 'Ride on my back, Grandpa, we will travel to Ngorongoro to the final resting place where all old males go. There is safety and water and gossip.' 'I am grey and frayed like you,' agreed Grandpa. 'But you can't go,' howled his granddaughter. 'Not without your teeth. It's not polite.'

Stones

I follow dry-stone walls
as mile after mile, they spread their history
each stone individual in feel, size and colour
built by gnarled and aching hands.
Like old stone houses, their thick walls
enclose secrets of lives lived and lost.
Stones are silent, they cannot gossip.

The Japanese have pet stones,
stroke them, whisper, confide in them,
give them personalities with names like Cyril.

Revolutionaries scream, hurl abuse, throw stones
that shatter glass, are weapons of rage.
There are those who sit stony-faced
mesmerised by iPad messages.
But stones are not immobile, they
slide along creek beds, tumble and crunch,
can kill in avalanche without remorse.
Stones may lay buried for centuries
or chat and clatter in aimless tidal voyage.

Sculptures of stone tell stories of heroes and heroines.
Gravestones portray facts of the dead after living.

Deceived By Appearances

Fruits of the Queen of the Dead
pomegranates – lustrous, rich,
mystical as the apple
that haunted Paradise.

Bound to the Underworld of Hades
Persephone beckons with ruby seeds
that glow in ripening summer sun
promising fertility, tranquillity and wisdom;
carried by desert caravans
pomegranates satisfy parched thirst
with juice that stained Persephone's lips,
the ancient fruit that enthralled
and all spirits who followed her
into the darkness.

Touch the antique leather of the fruit,
reflect on shadows, memories
that pull into the pain of self
bitter and sour as biting on the skin
blushing thick and hard beneath its crown
sheltering its jewels within.

The pomegranate tree strips leaves in winter
stands bare, resigned,
deaf to the song of the nightingale.

Watching Friends on a Wet Day

Two old men and their dogs
on a wide, cold beach
shuffle along in easy tempo

brown leaves hit my windscreen
aged and crumbled
brittle as promises

the slip slop of wipers
washes away regret
sun laces through the rain

dogs bark, their tails wagging
the men wave goodbye;
I feel their comfort in each other

Teapot

The teapot I hold was made in a back street by a potter in Batubulan. It is smooth as his skin and as round as his yellow-toothed smile. The bamboo handle was twined by a brown-eyed woman who has set out offerings for the Gods, intricate designs that will scatter under tourists' careless feet. I watch the woman push back her blue-black hair with long, strong fingers. Fingers that can wring a chicken's neck. Fingers that gently prepare the flowers for a body's final cremation. Fingers that now scatter ginger tea leaves into the pot. She pours boiling water ritually, fills the air with perfume, acrid but sweet as a funeral pyre.

She places the lid and twists it like the neck of the defeated rooster at the cockfight. She gestures that I share her tea. There is no sound except the pouring of tea, like a blessing.

Black Bear

We are lost
In a town near the Albanian border;
the street is rutted, narrow,
dark as evening falls.
Our battered Kombi bumps
towards a glowing light ahead:
it is a gypsy camp
of caravans and cooking fires.
Barefoot, bare bummed, dusty children
shriek and run around the flames
they jab sticks into a black bear, chained
to a pole and forced to stand.

My eyes are held by the bear,
She rocks passive at the taunts and jeers.
I long to soothe her black, matted fur,
bathe her dull, sad eyes,
soothe and stroke her damaged paws.

Was she captured from the Highlands,
Takht-e-Suliman and Toba Kakar?
Ensnared as a cub, was she taught
to dance for tourists?

Her eyes are sullen,
She looks malnourished.
Has she been forced onto hot coals
dancing while the fiddle music played?
She slowly rocks from side to side.

Dogs snap against the car,
a stone hits the windscreen hard.
We back the Kombi fast into the street.
I look back at the bear.
Soundless, she rears her head;
she has no escape.

Death is a White Syntax

The paper said that he had died.
But, it is him standing here, surrounded by eager
students.

He is older, greyer,
but still the whimsical, slow smile lights his face as
he reads words of his life and loves.

A husky drawl has replaced Aussie vowels,
now I remember old times
with friends, when we partied until dawn;

It is him.

He talks of syntaxicity and the message of the white space;

but I remember kisses in the front seat of the old Ford,
its grinding gears,
blue ball gown, running barefoot through the wet grass
the colour of the spaces thirty years ago.

White syntax.

The space between the lines.

The Black Hole of Three A.M.

The night is dark and still,
my body, a heavy dough of sleeplessness.
Thoughts thrash like moments
caught on barbed wire; itching eyes,
blind to half-wake possibilities.
I stare at the black silhouette in the corner,
a gentleman's serpentine armchair
resurrected from spiderwebs
and rats in the shed – its broken canes
now rewoven and patterned.

I remember dark-eyed patient women
weaving rattan from a Java forest,
their chairs for sale in Jakarta's market
with lychees, coiling cobras, monkey meat.

Three a.m. and memories flit like ghosts
in those timeless, half-lived hours
I have no ritual to explain the night.
If I sleep, I may disappear into the dark hole
of the Spiderwoman's womb.
I hear the grandfather clock bong another hour
while spent candles of thought melt and fuse.

Sudden screech of tyres rips into the dark,
a wind begins to hum across the sea.
Around the chair, shadows move against
its curves and pliant twigs. I rise, curl into my chair,
feel the cane against my bones, wait breathless
for the sun to rise.

Solitary Man

He stands, hands in pockets,
stares out over the ocean.
Walks the dog
to escape domestic walls
where anxieties circle.

He stands, hands in pockets,
stares at the ocean –
its depths
answer the unanswerable.

He stands, hands in pockets,
shelters under wattle bloom
that shrouds the dog,
friend of that solitary man

He stands hands in pockets,
stares at the ocean, breathes
the icy air, listens to yawning waves,
birds trembling their uncertain song.

Elephantidae Loxodonta Africana

I touch the folded skin
like grey-brown leathery parchment
covering a ponderous hulk
of power and trumpeting independence.
Elephantidae Loxodonta Africana
on dusty trails of the Serengeti
you swing a metronomic trunk
swish large and fan-like cooling ears
while you uproot, scatter small acacia
twirl anything green into a tiny mouth
twitch and itch and burn in beating sun
roll hugely in the dust.

Men kill the giant for its tusks –
ripped for trophies, aphrodisiacs
piano keys, carved opium boxes,
seals for the Emperor of Japan.
Throw the ivory dice against the elephant's foot –
ruby studded umbrella stand
in a New York department store.

Scattered

Painted plate,
old and secret as the woman
sitting in a backstreet shop
on a hot Singaraja day

Now fallen, it has shattered.
only memories remain of a joyful discovery:
smooth, heavy, cool to hold, a faded image
of painted Garuda bird ready for flight.

We haggle in Rupiah,
she quietly, firmly insistent,
then a final nodded agreement,
we drink tea as Bu wraps my prize.
Blessing each other, I retreat from
the quiet, dusty calm of her shop.

Now faces of old friends appear.
The joy of discovered friendships
but the shattering pain of their ends.
No gentleness in such going
of scattered ashes
like shards of my Singaraja plate.

The Silent Place

Hear the wind howl around harsh corners,
watch kestrels hover over a trembling sea,
feel the dry crackling of a wash
waltzing on a backyard line,
cut an apple's sheltering peel,
sing to a child's frustrated whine.

Then stand quiet, listen to the silence;

it deafens with a truth that few will listen for.
We choke the silent places with noise
to avoid the loud aloneness of us all.

It is hard to face the emptiness.

The Last Dahlia

My father prized and cherished dahlias,
Guatemalan flowers like burning sunrise.
Each morning in the strawberry garden,
smoking the day's first Capstan, a
checked blue dressing gown enfolding
his grey-haired chest, he stood.
Coughing, coughing,

In winter, dahlia tubers huddled
dark in the shed. He prepared
the roots, brown as the growth deep
in his lung, festering and crawling.
Breathing hard, he dug chilled earth
for spring.

When the circus came to town
he surveyed it imperiously, a conquistador.
Towing us kids, pushing the wheelbarrow,
he shovelled elephant turds bigger
than great, brown dinner plates, laying them
on his dahlia patch.

In summer neighbours eyed the glorious
suburban conquest. Plants like trees
upholding gold and crimson suns.
My father's Aztec *ecocotli*.

He cut the last dahlia in autumn,
putting its shouting pink in a vase,
hiding the shadow of my father's skin.
The tumour crept from lungs, to liver, to brain,
its poisonous tendrils choking.
The giant blushing dahlias
blazoned his final defiance.

Dancing With the Tide

Spread along the wide beach, a carnival of people
white, raw, pink, round, thin, bold
a circus of coastal gypsies, strangers
held together by the sea that tickles and torments –
squealing, laughing, splashing, choking,
restless, the tide mutters in endless rhyme.

They venture out, mad ones in a tinny boat;
thermos and a sandwich or two
and the smell of burley and the bait
and the lines and the squid jags –
eternal
fishing joy of an anticipated catch.
Land is soon far away, the swell torments.

Let the sea, grey and heaving, wash away sins;
fish and eels pick at bones.
Food for a carnival dancing at the edge.

The Lost Children of Bangkok

Round eyes black as ebony, still
as the stone lying by the tiny body –
child-unwanted, unnamed, unloved,
another piece of back street Bangkok trash.

They wander from the tribal hills
where girls have little worth.
The Karen, Kachin, Shaku, Chin,
the city is the lure that calls.
Olive skin, black, black hair and
almond eyes the colour of obsidian –
mountain virgins in the city
sell their unsoiled youth in Patpong bars
to sleezy tourists, older than their fathers,
who betel chew and grow the poppy.
Their whoring children send money
when the harvest fails.

No place for babies in this brutal world:
dark allies hide the dismal truths.

Blossom Time

It is raining hard. The hills
are caught in mist, a virgin's veil.
He ploughs heavy pounding the tractor,
blinded by the wet around, around
up, down, fingers chilled, head bent
feet aching in the cold.

Blossom glows on the black branches
of the almond trees – white
against grey. Fragile beauty bursts
from gnarled wood.

He blows on his fingers, rubs icy hands,
brings the tractor to a stop.
Leaning out, he touches the white petals
fine like her ivory skin.
Each year the almond blossom is a memory:
He hears the laughter of his daughter,
feels the wind that tossed her hair
as she rode with him and they harvested.

She had promised, 'Dad, when I get married
I'll wear blossoms in my hair.'
Now the white flowers warn of life's fragility
A wet night, a turn too fast…
The almond blossom, her funeral wreath.

The Power of Silence

The eagle, high, sweeps
across the sea, still as glass,
swoops fanning wings along
the rim of ancient sandhills.

The talons rip and hook, silently
embed into quivering fur
squealing bloody and defeated.
Grey carcass swinging, bird
soars into the ice-blue sky,
falling towards cliffs, ochre bare.

The eagle's silence,
the song of the powerful.

Tombstone, Arizona

I stand in the Bird Cage Theatre, where
Lillie Langtry sang, Fatima belly-danced.
Their ghosts still haunt the stage –
In the basement a poker game began in 1881
lasted eight years, five months and three days.
Johnny Ringo and Diamond Jim played their hand.

From the ceiling hung gold cages draped in red
where Margarita, 'Gold Dollar', posed,
with other 'soiled doves'. Whisky-soaked,
cowboys paid a silver dollar for a little love
I hear Lola Crabtree's laughter, the swish of gowns
and heavy men demanding service at the bar.
Feel bullet holes, one hundred and twenty-one in all,
shot by unhappy clients from colt forty-fives

Margarita, 'Gold Dollar', their photos shine –
hair piled high, smiling, coy, cream naked flesh,
laced-up boots, gloves and fans.
Under each bordello bed, a flowery chamber pot,
airless rooms, wardrobed, mirrored, with chair and corset stand.
No escape except in booze and laudanum
and finally carriaged in the Black Maria Hearse
to a Boot Hill grave alongside outlaws
gunned down by sheriff Wyatt Earp.
In the street, I watch Bo Jangles sing
and play the music of the bones.

Apple Pie

The dog moans in the kennel.
She turns the car onto asphalt,
grinding gears, sweat on the steering wheel,
dog hair on the seat.
She listens,
still hears his dog.
Closes the window, tight,
now only silence.

She drives wildly,
remembers apples, fallen apples,
picked up in autumn.
They walked in the orchard,
wicker basket dangling,
fingers touching,
silent together,
shoes scrunching on dry earth.

She will buy apples,
make his favourite pie.
Cinnamon, cloves, shortcrust pastry,
she will eat it all with cream,
watch TV very late
and eat potato chips and chocolate in bed.
No one there to make her feel guilty.

Before Full Moon

Frangipani and a blood-red rose –
roaring Ayung river down below echoing
the thud of water onto rice paddies
that layer upon layer jigsaw up the hill.
Bodies dot fields, calling 'Aheee'
as they start to reap the day;
small birds hang like kites
in air so heavy it stills the breath

Sickles glint as hills of bright green grass
are cut by men with gleaming bodies;
they hang on slopes like roots of banyan trees
and cut with slashing sweep into the earth.

The rapids of the Ayung snarl and lurch.
In peaceful shallows, daily baths begin
and shouts of cold on warmer skin
echo amongst frayed palms.
Mist rises from the valley,
cicada rhythm drowns falling frangipani
as white geese waddle to pasture
and the first cocks crow

The burnished plumes of birds shine,
preened before full moon
when silver claws will rip a sudden death –
the winning cock crows its triumph.

Criticism

Words like feathers
after a pillow fight
float in a sky the colour
of spilled, stale milk.
Drop to the hard, harsh earth
get lost in nervous weeds
of criticism, trampled
before a thought is born.

Eggshells

People of words
walk on eggshells,
wander into jungles
to follow serpents;
turn gourmet illusion
into indigestible fact,
create disquiet
where there has been indifference;
burn and scorch the blank page;
stumble into chaos,
light lanterns in the dark.

Once written
a thought cannot be unwritten.

Road Kill

Kangaroo Crossing,
warning sign on the highway
roos do not comprehend,
nor cars driven by town tourists.

Long feet, powerful legs, tails
so strong they swipe
and break men's bones.
Roos have no sense
of bitumen's danger.

Her sudden appearance shocks,
our national icon on the coat of arms,
leaping sudden from scrub
or harvested paddock,
into traffic; she collides
with screaming tyres.

She quivers, collapses on her side;
grey, quiet, movement stills.
A shocked driver feels his car's
crumpled carcass, thinks
of the kangaroo, its frozen leap
on the dollar coin in his pocket.

No More Vintage

Shining mellowed in the autumn sun
vines spread drunk and gaunt
their song of harvest ended.
Yellowed leaves defy grey skies,
drop by fence posts, lurching black and aged
their twisted wire no obstacle to kangaroos
exploring rows of sprightly cuttings
newly stretched across green acres
where once barley grew.

Tomorrow, they too may go.
Neat parcels of land for sale,
road signs and houses swallow
enchanted memories of harvest.

Moments

sailing boat
lurches through the sea
slapping water
hard against the prow

harvested barley
knitted rolls of hay
squat like giant puzzle pieces
gleaming in sun-kissed paddocks

girls giggle by the bus stop
chew gum loudly
hair long and gold
shining like loosely shredded silk

heavy bags bump against thighs
of hurrying shoppers
dodging bitumen bullies
who hunt for car parks

El Duende

We women follow the lure of the bandoneon
our song, the language of the tango.

Prowling through the restless night
we search for the lost spirit we failed to nurture.
Within a cursing web of pleasure we dance,
agitate and chant *mise en scène* together
with Marie de Buenos Aires, seduced
by memories conjured in the tango.

We hide in shadows, write our stories
on trees and chimney smoke
to remind us that once we were mothers.
Now seduced, corrupted, insulted
by the music of the bandoneon
and the hurdy-gurdy of the tango,
we are set adrift and have lost
El Duende, the spirit that lives in us,
the story of our self before our loss of innocence.

Sunday Benediction

They shamble like dark shadows
through veils of singing rain
those who seek solace and comfort
on still Sunday mornings
when the sea is flat and quiet,
gently sucking and pulling
at footprints of bare feet
inscribed like a last signature
in wet sand where the tide is low.
Grey sky outlines soft hills,
dragonflies tango.

On the bitumen sodden bike riders,
bodies hairless, oiled, lycra-muscled
streak by in an orange flash
whirring their way to purity and pain.

Backyard Bird

Colluricincla Harmonica

Grey shrike thrush hides its secret
beneath dung-coloured wings.
Pecks and claws for insects, beetle, even frogs
around logs and tree trunks, sharing
with his mate, a partner for life,
flies back to the same place year after year
to a nest of bark strips, course grass
but smoothly lined inside.

Ordinary, you say, but from this tiny bird
a song of sweet, ringing strength
stills the air such that Melba would weep.
High up on a branch, sound cascades
as pure as an opening almond blossom.

Solitary at Sea

They sit solitary at sea
water turning mango at sunset –
boat and man, a dark silhouette
below flocks of birds
skimming the sky

Taksu

Darkness hides grey fingers of the frangipani
silhouettes prahus clawing the beach
and the sacred banyan tree where bats hide.

Voices fill the dark, children chattering,
men's clove cigarette harsh laughter
and talk of cockfights at full moon –
bronze men like shadows
stand on the reef and pull nets
that glitter with fish from the black sea.

Their heads weighed with offerings
from symbols of life on earth,
women tread heavy across the sand
beneath palms rich with coconuts.
Their strong hands, smooth with oils,
dance in the soft air in greeting.

Listen to the night's pleasurable rhythm:
Gamelans play as ancient rituals begin
to inspire the spirit that dwells in shrines and temples
in the wilderness or tops of mountains,
while Balian tatakson calls down taksu
to shelter the soul's harmony.

Too Many Goodbyes

Last night the sun
bled across the sky –
she died as it set
with family around to say goodbye.
Fourteen years of caring,
fourteen years of loving
a long-haired German shepherd
our children christened Daisy.

Home to an emptiness –
a mat still warm
indented with her shape
a food bowl empty, a water bowl dry.
No welcome bark, a hollow quiet.

Now I grieve another friend
who has died today too soon,
too ill, too lost from her reality.
Numb with grief, I long
to hide in Daisy's long soft hair
feel her understanding.
But she is gone.
Memories are Band-Aids –
they cover the loss,
the hurt remains

Grandma's Garden

Freesias flower in gardens of old ladies'
their scent a grandma's perfume,
the misty smell of hope and place:
their funnel-shaped flowers the colour of clotted cream
on thin, delicate stems like young girls
waiting at a dance, cautiously demure.
Not like brazen modern girls in strapless gowns
of black with breasts pushed up and plumped…
boys who buy corsage flowers for their dates,
would not know the perfume of the freesia
a flower still combined in wedding bouquets.

A southern African native bulb,
one would expect a tough, wild flower
not a blossom so delicate it will easily bruise.
Its sweet fragile flowering
conjures memories of security and belonging.

Boy at the Bus Stop

Monday 4.04 p.m.
Tuesday 3.59 p.m.
Wednesday 4.00 p.m.
Thursday 4.03 p.m.

I watch him, boy in a wheelchair,
hunched in the bus stop shelter –
black-haired, long necked,
ears pink beneath a baseball cap.
Still, statue still, he stares,
smoke drifts like useless ambition.
Elbows red, eyes uneasy,
he studies the graffitied wall.

Trucks, cars, gleam and speed,
Commuters stand around him;
broad shouldered, stubborn chinned,
he is centre stage, rolls a cigarette.
No one speaks. One woman smiles.
A bus pulls in, city bound,
footsteps thrust against the bitumen.
Alone, he hunches, listens,
pulls on racing gloves,

spins into the traffic…Friday, 4.10 p.m.

Devil Mixed With Angels

Listen to the tango nuevo
from the back streets of Buenos Aires.
He flashes a knife, puts a gun
to the head of Piazzolla,
bandoneon player who
performs for ears not dance.

In the dark and heat, hear the accordion
sounds of devils mixed with angels;
Piazzolla's tango in Argentina
burns Bach's full-bodied allegro,
drowns Ligeti's ghostly discord
smothers Stravinsky's strident chords.

The violent Tanguedia triumphs.
It pours deep into the edgy places,
fires passion on this thick, dark night.

Argonauta Nodosa

Fossilised white eggshell
woven by an octopus,
its fragile body translucent,
a delicately formed
giant snail, now empty of life
once food for clumsy fur seals
along the rocky shoreline.

A perfect paper nautilus is prized:
beach combers hunt and wade in shallows,
cry in triumph at an undamaged shell.

I wander to a garage sale
round the corner one Sunday.
Amongst metal tools, old magazines,
potted plants, a paper nautilus
glows white and perfect

Paper nautilus now coils above shelves of books,
looks out at the swirling tides;
listen to the shell, transparent when the sun shines,
its echo of the sea touches
a mystery of ocean depths.
Some call it symbol of the spirit's growth.

White Crane

I watch the tall crane approach,
her wings gliding wide
and white low across the bitumen
'too low, too low',
I warn too late –
two long, black legs scrape
the silver bonnet of the car.
Bird and I reflect fear
in each other's eyes,
hers round and black,
mine, squinting blue.
She soars,
fluid as a harmony
pulsing towards the sea.

Monday morning and the traffic throbs,
my destination earthbound;
but our paths have crossed,
almost touched.

Sonnet For John

Wind blows the barley heads, a sea of grain.
Dawn breaks upon the snake inside the shed.
The farmer yawns, adjusts his aching frame
a shovel close, he lunges at the head.
The body writhes and headless, coils and rears;
he chops again, again, it shudders, still.
He harvests in the paddocks, hides his fear
the bank will take it all to pay the bill.
Old hat pulled low to shade an ageing face,
the farm is all he knows, each river bend.
Grandfather caught him yabbies in this place.
Four generations on this land will end,
farm work's a job his children now despise.
A curlew's call echoes his silent cries.

The Singer

The violins rained Mathis der Mahler
stabbing deep
into untouched places.

Brecht, Kurt Weill and Eisler
taunted through the Singer's mouth.
At ease, she stood, flaunting
in a black gown.
Madame, bar girl, Surabaja Johnny,
she became them all.

Soaked, we crept into the black night.
No one whistled a tune.

An Insubstantial Sweetness

They never picked gooseberries, raspberries, blueberries
but blackberries, large black berries
hung luscious each summer
between bitter, warring thorns on
bushes twisting like barbed wire alongside
farm fences and country roads.
They picked blackberries, collected them in
old billy cans and saucepans,
berries hidden beneath green, strong leaves
with thorns that cut and made them bleed.
Berries and blood, staining, as they
picked the juiciest and the biggest, blackest fruit.

A tradition until he was lured away
by a blackberry-eyed woman
who smelled of spices and sweet lychee.
While she bottled blackberry jam
another woman went gooseberrying, stealing her man
like a thief stealing clothes hanging out to dry.
Shining jars of jam blinked on quiet, pantry shelves,
with labels, blue-eyed wife, boiled and bottled
past the used by date.
Chekhov wrote of gooseberries, equated them
with luxury and self serving happiness.
Seamus Heaney's poem of blackberry picking
cries of their insubstantial sweetness
before the flesh turns sour.

One Day at Notre Dame

Quasimodo sits with me
hunched on the high bell tower.
He rings his beloved bells, calls
'Let me go with you for just one day.'
'I have no freedom to give,' I sigh.
Deaf, he cries, 'Let me be free!'
We munch baguettes, he weeps loud tears.
'Here,' I offer, 'wear my marguerites.'
'They smell of Esmerelda,' he chokes.
'She is sublime, I am grotesque.'
'True,' I nod and touch his monstrous hands.
Together we stroke gargoyles' ugly faces,
before he leaps into the clamorous sky.
Below, crowds call at my Pope of Fools,
Shout abuse he no longer hears;
only bells fill his silence with their song.

Mellow Season

The contented cluck of Alison's chooks
scrabbling amongst green scraps and bread
with bustle and peck and knowing nod.
Vines tum gold, their gawky limbs
silently shed brittle leaves.
The soil smells moist after soft rain.
A kestrel sweeps and hovers,
dives fast as a bullet, soars and karks
settles on the stobie pole as wind stirs.
The sea riffs and ripples loudly, leaves agitate
on restless melaleucas, tea trees and acacias,
their yellow blossoms scatter like confetti.
Daisy walks beneath, her shiny brown coat
covered like a bride who has said I do.
The sun slides into a mellow afterglow.

The Tamarisk

The tamarisk journeyed
from Abraham's biblical desert
across seas to far places:
Egypt, Pakistan, Australia,
to bring comfort and relief
for those living in emptiness.

Tiny flowers, clustered feathery,
pink and white on tough branches,
hard to burn, planted by Bedouins,
Jews for the next generation.

Abraham planted the tamarisk
for comfort, honey and shade.
Poets plant poems, that sometimes
flower in desert places.

Drown in Birdsong

I listen to birds,
their effortless song soars,
coloraturas of the trees.
I slush through muddy moods,
thoughts sink and drown,
words hang damp, pegged,
a poet's flapping laundry,
no wind, no sun to inspire its dance.
The rhythm of days falters,
crushed beneath news –
a daily press shouts
of cruel and powerful men.
The sea is still, vast,
my stroke becalmed
in the shallows.

The Housewife

She picks hibiscus buds in the still outside,
husband shaving, father snoring,
daughter whining, mother searching
for her teeth in the busy bathroom.
Moments of treasured quiet and birdsong
undemanding like family, the cacophony
of their needs, 'my lunch, my porridge,
have you fed the cat, where's my homework';
soon the olds will die, the kids mature and go,
egos polished like her furniture.
She balances the budget with his weekly wage,
he keeps enough for cigarettes and beer…
is no good with money, she has learned
on the farm through drought and locust plague.
Cooks the Barossa way, the strudel, sponges, roasts.
but now she's tired, life gets in the way,
to stop, to rest, smell the roses in a garden
she has made from dirt and clay; instead
she hangs the washing, pegs shirts and sheets
that swing and dance, round and round,
like all her dreams, going nowhere.

Sometimes She Understands the Right Thing at the Right Time

Picasso understood flesh on flesh –
the raw entwined bodies
heavy exposure of thighs…
not an easy picture to paint,
human sexual ecstasy – the sweat
sighs, groans, exultation of power.
Voice to voice, mouth to ear
bodies absorbed in the moment
of breath and musicality:
rhythm of hip and breast
no bed can hold the sun of their awakening
the song of their bodies
toes and fingers feeling
muscles moving in tempo.
No need to speak of love –
drown in the ocean of the moment
beyond the bones, listening
to the sense of things.

He painted the dangerous complications
in the essence of so little.

Roots

They run wild and wide
agapanthus blue
a crown of flowers on long, soft stems,
a bouquet of blossoms
defying wind and rain.

Roots run tough and long,
defy deep digging
resist eradication
like families, whose roots
knot through generations.

There is no say about our genesis,
red-haired, blue-eyed, short, long-nosed,
like the agapanthus old roots
will clutch, wherever we go,
defy who we see reflected in the mirror.

Sing My Poem

Dance to my poem
its tango and blues
songs of melancholy
in a rhythm of dream.
Gravel-voiced Louis,
the gruffness of Ella,
seduction of Sinatra
arousing the past, they smother
an uneasy truth of now
and long hours of smoky grey.
Sing my poem, bird, high
on a wire humming in the wind.
Lift with your trilling song
the wounded hope of my words.

Summer Evening

The kestrel sweeps in every evening.
She sees him nestle on the beam beneath the eves
where he watches across the sand as darkness falls.
His presence is a certainty now her life is full of doubt.
The peace of darkness cloaks her in its comfort –
she thinks of hawks, their shrewd awareness,
their bright, knowing eyes. They wear no watch
and keep no diary time, no mechanical device
halts their journey: instinct
guides their swoop and dive within a sky
stretching to infinity.
They need no gods to ward off fear;
in the perfumed dark she too can soar,
throw away constraints of daily grind.
Sometimes like the kestrel she is free.

The Children Sing

Ladybirds surf and huddle,
lost souls skimming on the tide.
The sun burns orange on the sea,
birds fly against mauve, mournful clouds,
ladybirds scuttle onto shore, scrabbling frantic,
spreading in a shimmering rug on the sand.

Face alight with joy, my daughter whispers
'Ladybird, ladybird, fly away home,
your house is on fire and your children are gone.'

They climb on her feet, fill her pockets,
measure hands for wedding gloves,
cover fingers, climb up arms,
desperate little *coccinellidae*
the Swedes call 'Virgin Mary's little hens,
tiny, racing legs tickling their good fortune
against soft skin tingling with surprise.

Our child is safe and loved as she sings
'Ladybird, ladybird, fly away home
your house is on fire and your children are gone.'

But there are children lost, countries of orphans
in Uganda, abducted children train to kill.
El Salvador, stolen children sell like chickens.
In Somalia, no parents, brothers, sisters, only orphans.
Rwanda butchered its lost children.
In Afghanistan, the instituted children sing,
'We are the white doves of peace.'
Ladybird, ladybird, fly away home,
your house is on fire and your children are gone.

Driftwood

These are mellow years
pruned by icy mornings
coloured in over ripe sunsets
spread like Persian rugs
their woven years of memories
no one now remembers.

Untouched for years
thoughts bleach like driftwood
half-buried knots, whitened curves,
the folds and humps remind
of limbs no longer long and lithe,
tormented by the cold
all the hurried days have dropped
silently as brittle leaves.

A Rose By Name

I know of those who cannot weep aloud,
who take their fears and sadness to the tomb
but hear the pain of others in the crowd.

I see each day their lonely heads are bowed
and joy is swept like dust before the broom.
I know of those who cannot weep aloud.

The damask rose is sensuous and proud,
its perfume lights the garden like the moon.
She hears the pain of others in the crowd.

My mother was a rose who sang and flowered
then curled up like an infant in the womb.
For she was one who could not weep aloud.

She rode a magic carpet through a cloud
but stopped her song when life sped out of tune,
no longer heard the pain within the crowd.

I watched her sad-eyed weave a dismal shroud.
I tried so hard to catch her fading bloom.
I know of those who cannot weep aloud
but hear the pain of others in the crowd.

www.ingramcontent.com/pod-product-compliance
Lightning Source LLC
Chambersburg PA
CBHW071035080526
44587CB00015B/2627